SMART PLYWOOD
BUYING GUIDE

AF173492

SMART PLYWOOD
BUYING GUIDE

Akhilesh Chitlangia
INDIA'S LEADING PLYWOOD EXPERT

Published Internationally by

Pendown Press
Powered by G Gullybaba꞉

PENDOWN PRESS

Powered by **Gullybaba Publishing House Pvt. Ltd.**,
An ISO 9001 & ISO 14001 Certified Co.,
Regd. Office: 2525/193, 1st Floor, Onkar Nagar-A, Tri Nagar,
Delhi-110035
Ph.: 09350849407, 09312235086
E-mail: info@pendownpress.com
Branch Office: 1A/2A, 20, Hari Sadan, Ansari Road,
Daryaganj, New Delhi-110002
Ph.: 011-45794768
Website: PendownPress.com

First Edition: 2021
Price:
ISBN: 978-93-90828-86-9

Layout Design: Pendown Press Publishing

Printed and bound in India by Thomson Press India Ltd.

CONTENTS

PRAISES

"I have known Akhilesh for many years now and he is always looking to add value to customers. This book is an extension of that – as a consumer it will add tremendous value for anyone looking to buy the right quality plywood."

– Pragat Dvivedi,
Founder - Ply Reporter,
India Interior Retailing, New Delhi

"Most of the time, clients just want to buy some Plywood and get on with the job. They do not realize that once woodwork is done, you are stuck with it for many years. An investment of half an hour or 40 minutes to read this book will be the best return you get from your new house."

– Architect Jatin Goel,
Architectural Concern, New Delhi

"This book is a must-have for anyone looking to get their interiors done. It is hard for homeowners like us to understand Plywood and what is right. This is where the book really helped us – We were able to make an informed decision and felt great about it."

– Rachna and Raghav Kheria,
Farinni Leathers Pvt Ltd, Kolkata

"With so many choices in the Plywood market, you never know what you are really buying. Not anymore – this book provides insight that is a MUST for anyone wanting good quality solutions for their woodwork."

– Architect Naveen Gandhi,
B.G. Associates, Jaipur

"There is so much misinformation about our industry; thank you, Akhilesh, for this amazing book to guide customers in the right direction."

– Vishal Jhawar,
Ply Samrat India Pvt Ltd,
Plywood Distributors, New Delhi

"This book will save you time, money, and most importantly, give you peace of mind. Beautifully illustrated concepts with easy-to-understand information. Thank you, Akhilesh, for writing this must-have book for every consumer in India looking to get their interiors done."

– Nitin Lunia,
Stencil, Plywood & Veneer Distributor, Bangalore

"I never knew so much went into getting the right plywood. The book is an Eye Opener, Simple, and a Must Have for homeowners getting their woodwork done."

– Vinay Agarwal,
Ex CEO, Independent Director and Business Coach

"The depth and simplicity of this book is amazing. Akhilesh's true intention for ensuring that each house has good quality plywood is truly reflected in this book."

– Akshar Yadav,
Creator of Get Overbooked, New Delhi

INTRODUCTION
FROM THE AUTHOR

Looking for good Plywood for your home? This may seem like a very simple question, but the answer involves lots of factors and considerations. I mean, of course, you want good Plywood for your home. You want your woodwork to last forever. You want your loved ones to feel comfortable and enriched in the vicinity of the woodwork.

But how do you make sure that you have got the right Plywood for the job? Want to know the insights and secrets known only to the experts or people who deal with Plywood and Block boards day in and day out so that you can make the right choice?

Then this book is definitely for you. The purpose behind writing this book is to help you understand the dynamics of Plywood and how you can add decades to the durability of the woodwork that you plan to get done inside your home or office by making some educated decisions.

One of the biggest reasons why you must read this book carefully is that if you implement some of the suggestions mentioned in the book, you can:

- Save a ton of time on maintenance and getting the work redone.

- Save lots of money in the long run because you will require fewer or even no repairs or replacements.

- Enjoy peace of mind knowing that your woodwork or your furniture is going to be with you for a very long, long time.

Trust me; it will be time well spent. Remember that the woodwork that you get done is not just a piece of wood. The cupboards, the shelves, the furniture, everything you get made becomes a part of your family. Your family will create memories using these structures. You do not want to give them unstable memories.

Besides giving you valuable information on Plywood, I have also included some insight to help you understand how wood is more beneficial for construction purposes than cement and steel. You can skip this information if you are in a hurry and straightaway refer to the relevant parts that deal with Plywood.

Hello, my name is Akhilesh Chitlangia, and I have been in the Plywood industry for the past eleven years. I joined my family legacy business immediately after completing my graduation, and ever since then, the wonders of wood, especially Plywood, have never ceased to amaze me.

Why this book on Plywood? The choice you make when selecting the right Plywood for your interiors will have a lifelong impact on you.

When I joined the family business, my father told me something that my grandfather had told him, "A home is a dream that needs to come true. People build homes with years of their hard-earned money, saving a little every year. It is a very aspirational yet emotional bond for every Indian. Therefore, we must ensure our customers always get the very best."

When you get woodwork done inside your home, you are constantly interacting with that woodwork. Whether it is the doors and windows, the paneling, the shelves, the study table for your kids, the beds in the house, your dining table, or other places where woodwork is required,

Plywood becomes a part of your life. You and your family create memories around the woodwork, sometimes, without even realizing it.

Despite being such an essential part of your life, there is a lot of misinformation about wood in general and Plywood in particular.

Plywood is extensively used. You see Plywood in action wherever you go, whether at home, someone else's house, or even a commercial place or an office. The Plywood industry has a turnover of Rs.30,000 crores in India every year. Unfortunately, only 20% of Plywood comes from the organized sector. It means 80% of the Plywood available in the market does not guarantee quality and durability, and consequently, most consumers feel disillusioned.

The book is organized into different chapters. Although there is an underlying theme that unfolds a story through the individual chapter, every chapter stands independently. So, if you feel that you need only a particular type of information for your Plywood needs, jump straight to that chapter and obtain the information.

I hope this book enriches you regarding the choice of Plywood for your woodwork. You are welcome to contact me if you need more details.

Section A

ABOUT WOOD
AND YOUR OPTIONS

Chapter 1

WHY WOOD IS THE BEST CHOICE FOR YOUR INTERIORS

Many people mistakenly think that wood is less durable and less sustainable than materials like cement, concrete, and steel. Whereas all the materials have their pros, wood comes with extraordinary properties that are not available in other materials. For example, do you know that wood gives you 5X more insulation than concrete and 350X than steel? This is precisely why wood is used to make houses and buildings in cold climates, especially in the US.

Also, contrary to popular belief, wood is less environmentally harmful than cement and other construction materials. Why, may you think? Are we not cutting trees to get construction-grade wood?

Yes, we do cut down trees to get wood, but these trees can always grow back. Most of the commercial wood used for construction purposes is obtained from trees grown to generate commercial wood. An average tree from which wood is obtained can grow in 15-20 years. Some even in 7-10 years. In addition, the carbon footprint of wood-based products for many construction applications is far lower than other alternatives.

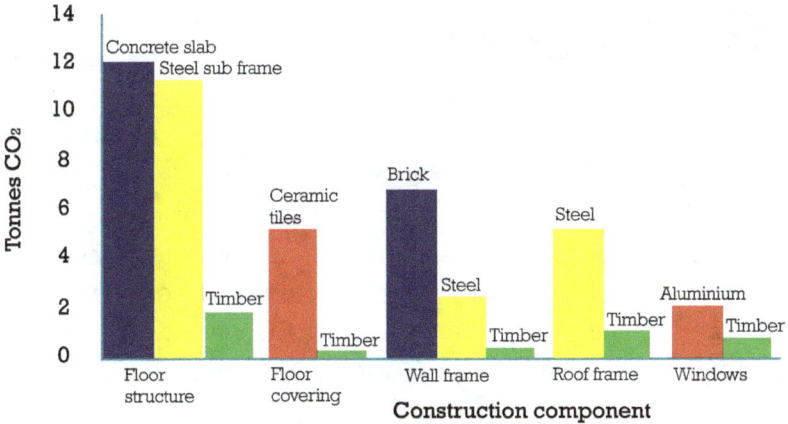

Figure 1 Source: Impact of Forestry Products on Climate Change Mitigation in India; International Journal of Applied Science and Technology; Vol. 4,No. 7; December 2014. Greenhouse Gas Emissions from the Manufacture of Different Building Components in a Family Home

Also, no harmful chemicals or heavy machinery are used when you grow wood for commercial use (or any other purpose). Want to grow a tree? Simply sow a seed or sapling on a decently fertile piece of land, water it regularly, and make sure that it is not eaten by animals or insects, and within a few years, you have a healthy tree for yourself without any side effect. There are many ways you can rotate your saplings so that you always have a healthy supply of wood.

Figure 2: Trees can be restored on Earthy in a few years and do not take up any substantial resources

Compared to this, the land that is used for mining to get cement or copper, or aluminum may lay waste for decades or even centuries. Also, to run mining operations, the local flora and fauna are badly damaged. Many international NGOs working in the field of environment preservation recommend wood-based construction. For example, the Forest Stewardship Council (FSC) is an American body and considered the Gold Standard to certify forest-based sustainable products. It highly recommends using wood for construction purposes. It is always advisable to go for wood-based products that a certified by agencies like the FSC.

Figure 3: Hadimba Palace in Manali, built in the 16th Century, is made completely of wood.

Is wood durable? Does it not get eaten by termites or begins to corrode or decompose? It depends on the quality of the wood. Most wood species do not corrode easily, and many varieties of wood are naturally termite resistant.

Think about it - houseboats used extensively for centuries have stood on water for generations and never had an issue. Then, there are some ancient buildings made of wood that still survive after centuries. Yes, centuries. Take, for example, the Hadimba Palace in Manali that was built in 1553 A.D. In Japan, the Horyuji Temple was constructed nearly 2000 years ago, and it is still intact and is a major spiritual attraction. The Rumtek Monastery in Sikkim was built in 1730 A.D. Many houses in the United States were built before or during the Civil War, and current generations are still using them. It is a misconception that wood gives away faster compared to other construction materials.

Figure 4: Horyuji Temple, in Japan, built in 7th Century is the worlds oldest Wooden Structure building and still standing tall to this day.

So, yes, when properly used, wood can be quite solid and can serve you for multiple decades and centuries.

Contemporary developments in wood making

Is wood always used as it is? Not necessarily. Maybe until a few decades ago, there was no other option but to use wood as it is with some modifications (for example, Plywood has multiple layers), but nowadays, at least in the past 10-15 years, there have been massive innovations in wood products. For example, in London, an entire 11 story building has been built without using steel and cement. They have used an engineered wood product called cross-laminated timber (CLT). Many such wood varieties are being created. There is even news of glass made of wood.

In India, we are still using the age-old varieties of wood, but as I have mentioned above, it is all about using quality wood for your woodwork, and provided you get your wood through proper channels, you can enjoy long-lasting solutions at home as well as at your workplace.

Chapter 2

WHAT ARE THE WOOD OPTIONS FOR YOUR INTERIOR WOODWORK?

Woodwork is not something that you can do casually. Even if spending money is not an issue, there can be lots of inconveniences. The woodwork inside your home (or office), unknowingly, becomes an integral part of your life. Just imagine, if something goes wrong with your woodwork (like a termite attack), taking all your woodwork out and then going through the entire hassle of getting everything fixed again. Your life could be turned upside down for many months.

Therefore, it is always advisable to choose your wood after careful consideration.

There are plenty of materials available today for your woodwork solutions. Each comes with its advantages and disadvantages. The essential thing is to use the right product for its intended use.

Here is a summary of the various options you have:

Plywood

Plywood is the most commonly preferred option for long-lasting woodwork for the last six decades in India. It is the best option due to its strength and durability.

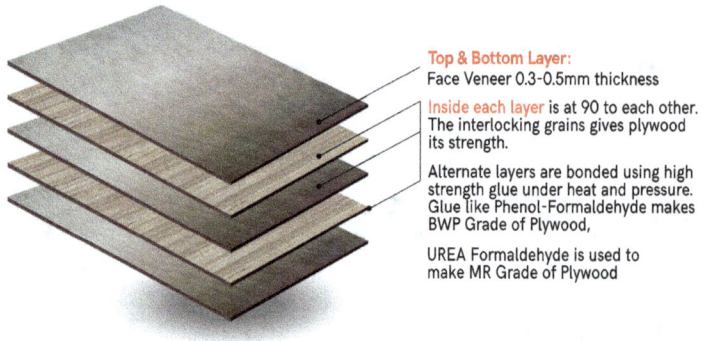

Top & Bottom Layer:
Face Veneer 0.3-0.5mm thickness

Inside each layer is at 90 to each other. The interlocking grains gives plywood its strength.

Alternate layers are bonded using high strength glue under heat and pressure. Glue like Phenol-Formaldehyde makes BWP Grade of Plywood,

UREA Formaldehyde is used to make MR Grade of Plywood

Note:
Each layer of wood veneer should be seasoned and have moisture level between 8%-12%. High quality Plywood are also treated for protection from insects such as termites and borers.

Plywood is like a multi-layered sandwich: sheets of wood veneer are arranged, 90° to each other, and then compressed and bonded under heat and pressure using a resin. This 90° arrangement makes them many times stronger than the actual, inherent strength of the wood.

Plywood also has a high screw holding strength, is an eco-friendly option, and comes in various thicknesses ranging from 4mm to 25mm.

Advantages	Disadvantages
Very Strong and Durable	Not to be used outdoors
Wide Range of Thicknesses (4mm to 25mm)	Unorganized sector is large, and hence it is easy to purchase the wrong product
High Nail & Screw Holding strength	Plywood cannot be exposed to wet or moist weather for an extended period.
Easy to Install & Shape	
Treated to be Termite Resistant	

Blockboards

Blockboards are complementary products to Plywood and not a direct substitute. Blockboards are best for vertical applications such as wall **paneling and cupboard shutters.**

Blockboards are made with solid wood batons and are the closest to solid wood in terms of construction. Blockboards are available in limited thicknesses – 16mm to 25mm.

Due to the unorganized sector, there are a lot of low-quality boards being sold in the market. We need to ensure that Blockboards are made from treated and seasoned timber for longevity and insect resistance. As it is hard to know this, trust a branded source.

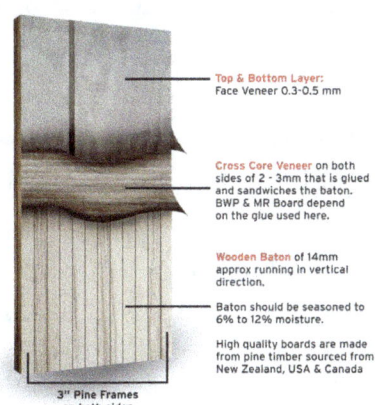

19 MM BLOCKBOARD

Top & Bottom Layer: Face Veneer 0.3-0.5 mm

Cross Core Veneer on both sides of 2 - 3mm that is glued and sandwiches the baton. BWP & MR Board depend on the glue used here.

Wooden Baton of 14mm approx running in vertical direction.

Baton should be seasoned to 6% to 12% moisture.

High quality boards are made from pine timber sourced from New Zealand, USA & Canada

3" Pine Frames on both sides

Advantages	Disadvantages
High Vertical Load Bearing Strength	Not as versatile as Plywood
Dimensionally stable and less prone to bending on vertical applications	Thickness limitation – available only in 16mm, 19mm, 25mm
Lighter in weight	Difficult to judge the quality of material used to make block boards

Are there substitutes for Plywood?

Can you completely replace Plywood with another substitute? Some products are there in the market, including MDF, Particle Boards, and WPC, which stands for "wood plastic polymer composite."

They are recent innovations, and they definitely have their advantages. But you must keep in mind that they are available in the market only where there is a dearth of good quality Plywood. You can call them the poor cousins of Plywood. When it comes to quality, strength, and durability, they cannot compete with Plywood or even with Blockboards, for that matter.

Hence, when it comes to recommending the best material for woodwork, I always recommend Plywood and Blockboards.

Why is Plywood superior to other alternatives?

These days MDF is being used a lot, especially as a good alternative to low-quality Plywood. It offers better uniformity compared to low-grade Plywood. Is it a good replacement for Plywood? Yes, if you are not concerned with good quality Plywood, and no, if you are. Quality

Plywood gives you superior strength, better screw holding capacity, durability, and far greater moisture resistance than MDF.

What about particle boards? In terms of durability, they are even worse than MDF.

WPC is comparatively better. It is immune to termites. This makes it a good option in extremely high moisture areas. Compared to particle boards, it is weaker but costlier. Since there is a high content of plastic, it does not decompose easily, and for the same reason, environmentally, it is not a healthy product.

Below is a short summary of each product.

MDF

Medium Density Fibreboard is made from wood chip particles that have been ground down to its fibre and bonded using a resin under high temperature and pressure. As it is made from wood chip particles and not solid wood sheets, MDF is inferior in strength and durability. In addition, MDF is known to swell at the slightest increase in moisture. MDF also tends to give a foulodour when exposed to extreme

Figure 5: Medium Density Fibreboard (MDF) has a lot of sawdust and chemicals sprayed into the air while cutting. This is harmful to those exposed to it.

climatic conditions,especially in high temperatures and moisture. This is due to the excessive chemicals used on bonding these boards, thereby making the product not safe for humans in general. In addition, while cutting MDF, there is significant sawdust which increases pollutants and is harmful to human lungs; if necessary, precautions are not taken.

MDF is gaining a lot of market share in India due to its lower price and smooth finishing, but for high quality, long-lasting woodwork, MDF is not recommended.

Particle Board

Particle Boards are made from wood chip particles similar to MDF but without grinding them down to their fibre. As a result, Particle Boards are stronger than MDF; however, Particle Board does not have dimensional stability, i.e., it is prone to bend and warp easily. Particle Boards are preferred by OEM, making lower-budget kitchens and furniture due to lower cost.

Figure 6: Pre-laminated Particle Board is gaining popularity in low-budget kitchens due to its low cost. These boards come with a different lamination on both sides, making it easier for installation, but overall quality and durability are very low.

Wood Plastic Composites/ WPC

Made from a mixture of Plastic and Wood Particles (or just PVC Plastic without any wood particles), WPC is a solution for areas that have high termite infestation issues. The product is expensive compared to even Plywood and has a lower screw holding capacity. Made from PVC, high-quality boards are rare in India and have very low durability in the long run. Also, these boards are not recyclable and add to environmental hazards over the long run.

Figure 7: Good quality WPC in India is very rare and extremely expensive. We usually find a PVC Foam Board that has a high tendency to buckle with prolonged usage.

Here is a tabulated comparison of Plywood, Blockboards and all the other options and grades available for your upcoming woodwork.

Table 1: Comparison of Plywood, Blockboards, and other Options available for woodwork

	High Quality Plywood & Block Boards	Low Quality Plywood & Block Boards	High Density MDF	Regular MDF	Particle Board	WPC/ PVC Foam Board
Overall Durability	Very High	Medium	High	Low	Low	Low
Screw Holding Strength	Very High	High	Medium	Very Low	Medium	Very Low
Termite Resistance	High	Low	High	Medium	Medium	Very High
Ecological	Very High	Medium	Medium	Medium	Medium	Very Low
Health	High	Low	Low	Low	Low	Very Low
Moisture Resistance	Very High	High	High	Low	Very Low	High
Load Bearing	Very High	Medium	Medium	Low	Low	Very Low
Cost	₹₹₹₹	₹₹	₹₹₹	₹	₹	₹₹₹₹₹

Chapter 3

ENVIRONMENTAL AND HEALTH IMPACT OF WOOD-BASED PRODUCT

As a concerned citizen, you are obviously worried about using sustainable materials. In the introductory chapter, I have explained that wood is a much better option than other materials because it is renewable. Yes, some wood varieties take years to grow. Still, many options are available these days where trees can grow and can be turned into construction material within 7-10 years.

Compared to this, if you use concrete or plastics, they can cause irreparable damage to the environment.

Having said that, when it comes to using wood (even in the form of Plywood), we are naturally concerned about the depleting forest cover. People all over the world are worried about vanishing flora and fauna. There has been excessive logging in many parts of the world. Many governments have imposed restrictions against excessive tree cutting, including in north-east India, where restrictions were imposed in 1996. Burma, a major source of private material, imposed restrictions in 2014 to protect its forests.

Yet, there are some ways you can use Plywood and at the same time put less strain on the forests. You can make sure that you obtain your Plywood from FSC certified suppliers. The Forest Stewardship Council certification is given by an American Body that routinely audits organizations that obtain wood material following sustainable practices. In most of the cases, these organizations plant more trees than the log to obtain wood.

Chemical footprints and emissions

Synthetic resins used for Plywood are made of formaldehyde, a known carcinogenic (has cancer-causing properties) and can have long-term harmful effects. How do you make sure that you buy Plywood that is as harmless as possible for you and your loved ones as well as the environment?

Look for E1 & E0 grade wood products. These norms are set by the European Union to supervise how much formaldehyde is used in wood products. Both E1 & E0 are safe for human exposure.

Section B

HOW TO SELECT GOOD QUALITY WOODWORK FOR YOUR INTERIORS

Chapter 4

THE CHALLENGE OF BUYING THE RIGHT QUALITY PLYWOOD FOR YOUR INTERIORS

Now we come to the crux of this book. You want to select the best quality Plywood for your upcoming woodwork, whether for your home or office.

Coming across good quality Plywood is not easy, though. I am not saying that most of the Plywood available in the market is of inferior quality. The Plywood industry in India is around Rs.30,000 crores per annum, but sadly, as mentioned above, only 20% of it comes from the organized sector.

You face challenges at multiple levels. You never know who the genuine sellers are. It is very difficult to tell if the Plywood that you are purchasing is genuine or not. Branded or not,anyone can publish anything one feels like on a Plywood board and claim that it is the brand name.

Since the unorganized sector dominates 80% of the market, it is quite easy to land up with inferior quality Plywood when you do not have the correct information.

Plywood Industry in India

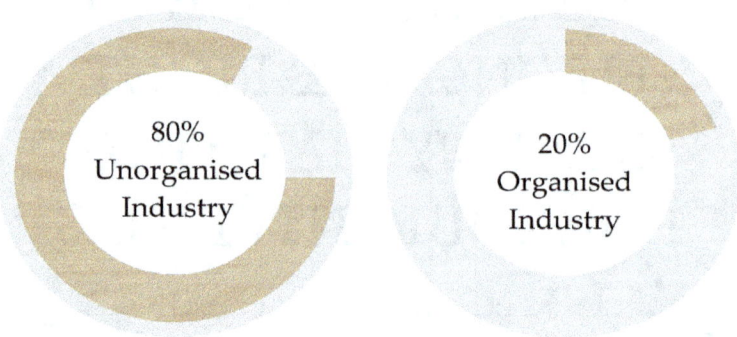

The good news is that you are reading this book, and I am sharing insights with you that will empower you to choose the most appropriate Plywood for your woodwork.

Understandably, someone who is not constantly dealing with Plywood may find it hard to distinguish between good quality and inferior quality Plywood. This is where this book can help you to choose like an expert.

Is it worth spending so much time? I can understand if you have such thoughts in your mind. After all, you simply want to buy some Plywood and get on with the job. But keep this in mind: once you have got the woodwork done, you are stuck with it for many years. Repeat that for many years. Half an hour or 40 minutes spent reading this book will save you days, even weeks of your precious time, and thousands of valuable rupees.

Chapter 5

SHOULD YOU BUY BRANDED OR LOCAL/ UNBRANDED PLYWOOD AND BLOCKBOARD?

Frankly, this is a difficult question, especially if you do not know the implications of buying unbranded Plywood and Blockboard.

Hence, what I am sharing here with you, pay close attention to it. Sure, you may get lots of advice from contractors, interior designers, architects, and even family and friends, but I am sharing insights that I have acquired after spending many years in the industry.

With 80% of the industry being unorganized, there is a massive variation in the price and quality available in the market. The price of 19 mm, commercial-grade

Plywood, can range between Rs.100 per square feet (premium brand) to Rs.30 per square feet (low quality and unbranded).

Hence, it is very easy to fall into the trap of "cheap price" and "easy availability." Difficult to beat, no?

How do you decide then? The choice needs to come from you. Do you want cheap Plywood for your interiors? Do you want Plywood that may swell, break or become termite-infested within a year or within a few years? Do you want to go through the hassle of getting the entire woodwork done again? Are you worried about the safety of your loved ones? Are you looking for accountability and guarantee in case something goes wrong with your wood?

Your answers depend on what type of Plywood and Blockboard you go for, for your upcoming woodwork. Below I am listing a few reasons why you should go the extra mile and stick with the 20% (and seemingly costlier) organized sector instead of the unorganized sector.

Better quality

What exactly is better quality? Better quality means durability. Quality Plywood and Blockboard are strong and durable. They are water-resistant. They are termite-resistant. They come with stronger nail-holding capacities. They come with after-sale support in case something goes wrong. They are not treated with harmful chemicals. They are going to adorn your interiors for many years, even many decades.

Sure, you can go with cheaper versions that are not branded. That is entirely up to you. After all, you are making a choice for your loved ones. Whether you want to give them the best or anything that comes in front of you, it is entirely up to you.

More versatility

Good Plywood and Blockboard (branded) are sturdy and can be used in different applications and shapes. They come with varying strengths, textures, and qualities that enable you to go beyond perceived capabilities. These capabilities are not available with unbranded and low-quality Plywood and Blockboard.

Quality assurance certificates

As mentioned above, these certificates can signify that you are getting your Plywood and Blockboard from reputed suppliers. They also ensure that you are getting environment-friendly products that are not harmful to you and your surroundings. They also ensure that your interiors are devoid of harmful microbes.

Borer and termite treatment

It is preferable that your products are not treated with chemicals excessively. Still, certain resin treatments ensure that they are borer (a variety of beetles that infest wood and wood products) and termite resistant. You do not get this safety in unbranded wood products.

Superior after-sales service

You may right now feel that after you have purchased Plywood and Blockboard, you may not require after-sales service, but the truth is that you will! You will recognize its importance once you are looking for support and replacements and you are unable to trace your supplier.

Ecologically and environmentally friendly

The raw material for branded Plywood is generally procured from legal, sustainable sources. In addition, during manufacturing, low formaldehyde emission resins are used; therefore, you get a product that is environmentally stable and not harmful for you and your family.

Chapter 6

MYTH OF BRANDED PLYWOOD BEING EXPENSIVE

It is a misconception that you are saving a lot by going for unbranded, inferior quality Plywood and Blockboard.

What is your entire budget for interior construction? 65 lakhs? 100 lakhs? Do you know for a 3 BHK house, the overall difference between a branded and unbranded (local) Plywood is Rs.65,000 to Rs.100,000? That is merely 1% of your total cost. Is it worth it, especially when the branded option gives you much better quality, durability, reliability, and above all, assurance and support?

Figure 8: Poor Quality Plywood resulted in Termite Infestation

In isolation, going for unbranded wood products may seem like a logical decision. After all, you are paying less, and at least right now, in the near future, you are not going to face any problem. But again, as I have explained

Figure 9: Poor Quality Plywood resulted in Termite Infestation that ruined Kitchen Interiors

above, how much are you actually saving compared to your overall interior construction, and, again, is it worth it?

Are all unbranded Plywood and Blockboard bad? No. There may be many ethical and hard-working manufacturers in the unorganized sector due to various unavoidable reasons. But it's like taking a chance. Remember that you do not get your interiors done regularly – in many cases, it is a once-in-a-lifetime investment. Why make compromises just to save a little?

I will give you a small, personal example. One of my customers, Mr. Manohar Shah (name changed to protect privacy), is a small business owner, and he was getting his kitchen renovated. To save costs, he forced his contractor to use unbranded Plywood sold by a nearby retailer who promised waterproof and termite-proof material, with even a 50-year warranty.

The woodwork did not last even for a year. It swelled fast. It got infested with termites. Because of the inferior quality of Plywood, even the additional work that he had gotten done got spoiled. Now Mrs. Shah, for whom the kitchen was the most important part of her daily routine, goes without saying, was extremely unhappy with this development. The couple would routinely call and visit the local supplier trying to claim their investment, but they did not receive any claim or support from the supplier. Instead, they wasted nearly three months fighting with the supplier and fighting amongst themselves.

Eventually, Mr. Shah, on his wife's insistence, purchased branded Plywood and got the entire kitchen redone. He spent almost four times what he intended to save by going for a cheap Plywood version. That, however, was not the heaviest price that he paid. Instead, it was the strain in his relationship at home that was the costliest.

Chapter 7

TERMITES – THE ETERNAL ENEMIES OF YOUR WOOD-BASED PRODUCTS

In the introduction, I promised that I would share some secrets on how to save your woodwork from termites who love to devour anything wood and turn it into dust. Many dreams have been turned to dust by these tiny, white ants that invade your woodwork like marauding armies.

I have been especially fascinated by termites because, given the right condition, they will always attack your wood and destroy it completely if you do not take precautions. They are a major cause of many wooden constructions being destroyed, sometimes complete establishments. I have visited multiple sites to witness the ruination they can wreck personally.

You can deal with an enemy better if you know it properly. Let's do that first.

What are termites, and how do they damage wood?

Do you know that termites are one of the most destructive pests in the world? Properties worth billions of dollars are destroyed by termites every year.

Figure 10: Termites are usually found in the soil (not always) and feed on wood in high moisture conditions. They look like white ants and can destroy wood-based products in a matter of days.

Since they look like ants, they are often called white ants, but they are not ants, and even the physical disposition is different from ants. They can eat anything they can get hold of, but they especially love wood. They thrive in high moisture conditions so, if there is a chance that there is moisture in your woodwork, you need to be wary of a termite attack.

How to keep termites at bay?

Termites do not like dry areas. Hence, if you can make sure that as much moisture as possible is drawn out of your wood, you can avoid termite infestation to a great extent. There are some excellent quality engineered wood products available from which moisture is drawn mechanically. Wood veneer and exposure to heat can reduce the inherent moisture within the wood by 8-12%. This helps you build a natural defense against termites.

Additionally, Plywood and Blockboard can be run through chemical treatment that makes your wood termite resistant.

What precautions should you take before the woodwork?

Sometimes, no matter how well your wood has been treated before you use it for your woodwork, the surroundings are good termite breeding grounds. Hence, before you begin your woodwork, make sure that

- The soil on which the construction is carried out is free of termites and their eggs.

- There are no termites and their eggs on the flooring of your house or your workplace.

- Regular treatment is done to keep termites away.

- Leaks that can give rise to dampness and excessive humidity are taken care of promptly.

- Wooden furniture is not frequently placed on the soil that may carry termites or their eggs.

Figure 11: Before construction begins, soil should be treated

- Only treated materials are used for woodwork – with resin that repels termites.

Figure 12: Ideally the soil should be without any Termite

Figure 13: Before flooring is done, a termite treatment must be carried out

Figure 14: In case of using solid timber, ensure it is properly treated to be termite resistant

Figure 15: Get leaks fixed at the earliest. Prolonged exposure to moisture results in a termite attack on your woodwork

Additional advice: Do not purchase your Plywood and Blockboards from multiple vendors. Stick to a single supplier who is reputed and can be easily traced. This is because later, if you face problems with the quality of the wood, you know whom to approach. Otherwise, if you deal with multiple vendors, they will keep pointing fingers at the other vendors, refusing to help you.

Pay attention to "under the hood" when it comes to guarantees and warranties

When you purchase your Plywood or block wood, the supplier may claim that you are getting a 15-year, or a 21-year, or even a 100-year warranty.

Let me share a secret with you: provided you are going for good quality Plywood or block wood, the only problem you will face is a termite attack. The unorganized sector does not even give you warranties and guarantees.

Hence, if your supplier offers you a warranty, make sure you go through the fine print. Specifically, **ask if they cover termite infestation.**

This is my advice as someone who has been selling good grade Plywood for years: ask your supplier if he gives you a guarantee against termites for many years. This can give you a good indication of whether the manufacturer has treated the wood to make it termite resistant or not. Of course, even if the wood has been treated, you will need to take the precautions mentioned above.

Section C

IDENTIFYING THE RIGHT PRODUCT FOR YOU

Chapter 8

VARIOUS TYPES OF PLYWOOD

Let us find out what types of Plywood are available in the market.

The best grade Plywood is made of a single high-density homogeneous timber. It means, the same species of wood is used throughout the production. These species can be Eucalyptus, Gurjan or Birch,Beech, just to name a few.

Material homogeneity has many benefits. It gives you a uniform look. It provides you dimensional stability. There is an overall evenness. Since the fibers of the wood are the same throughout, the Plywood is sturdier than other varieties.

Please remember that the rarer the wood type or the species, the pricier your Plywood will be. There are multiple varieties of Plywood available in India. Some have mixed raw materials (but usable nonetheless), and some have a single type of wood.

- Gurjan Plywood
- Hardwood Plywood
- Mixed hardwood Plywood
- Alternate Plywood
- Poplar Plywood
- Birch Plywood
- Beech Plywood
- Rubberwood Plywood

These are the most prominent varieties.

Let us go through some helpful information about these varieties of Plywood so that you have the upper hand when you are weighing your options.

Gurjan Plywood

It also has a sister species called Keruing.

Gurjan is primarily found in the tropical forests of Myanmar and Indonesia. Due to relentless logging, the governments of these countries have imposed restrictions, which often makes it difficult to get this variety of Plywood. It takes around 40-50 years for a Gurjan tree to mature and become appropriate for logging.

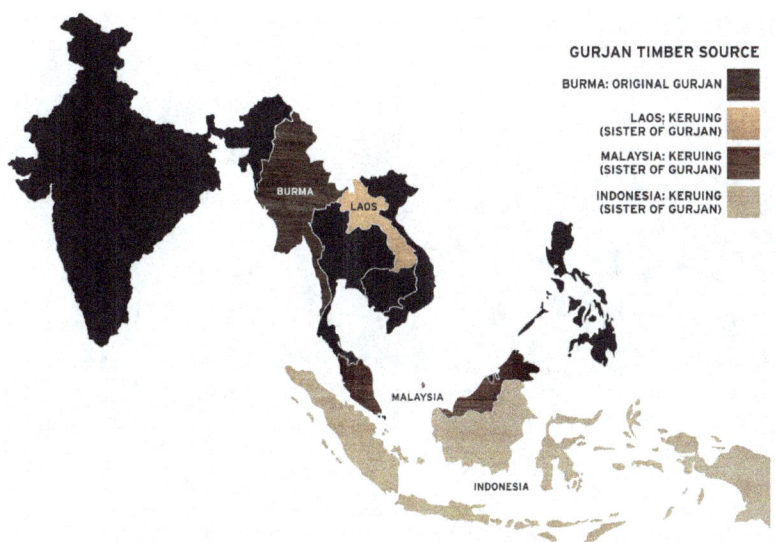

Figure 16: Gurjan Wood comes from Burma. Its sister specie, Keuring comes from other parts of Southeast Asia and is usually passed off as "original" Gurjan.

You do not often get the pure Gurjan Plywood. It usually is a mix of another variety that is visually like Gurjan, mostly hardwood. In most cases, the top layer is Gurjan, but the filling inside is of another variety.

100% Gurjan Plywood is certainly available, and you can expect to pay at least Rs. 140/sq ft++ (January 2021 prices) for a 19 mm Plywood.

Is there a way of finding whether you are purchasing genuine Gurjan Plywood? Yes. You will need to send it to a lab.

My take: Very reliable. Durable and solid. Go for Gurjan Plywood if budget is not a constraint.

Hardwood Plywood

Figure 17: Hardwood Plywood usually (not always) has a reddish appearance and uniform color all across. Remember to cut the Plywood and check the inside color well.

This is one of the most widely used Plywood varieties in India. It is made of eucalyptus trees, more commonly known as Safeda, primarily grown in Uttar Pradesh, Uttarakhand, Haryana, and Punjab. The wood is also imported from Indonesia and Malaysia.

Eucalyptus is a high-density, robust wood, and since it grows in plenty in India, it is well suited to the Indian climatic conditions. The good thing about Eucalyptus is that the tree attains its maturity in 8-10 years.

Eucalyptus needs to be treated before using to ensure high-quality Plywood is made. Not all factories can afford the machine required for the proper treatment. Hence, it is usually the organized sector that provides high-quality hardwood Plywood made from Eucalyptus.

When made from unseasoned or immature Eucalyptus; Hardwood Plywood tends to crack, delaminate, warp or bend, and have an uneven thickness, which affects the longevity and durability of your woodwork.

My take: Good value for money as long as you get it from a reliable source. Good quality Hardwood Plywood is what you should be considering for your home interiors.

Alternate Plywood

This category of Plywood is made of two timber species–hardwood and softwood. Eucalyptus and Poplar are the most common combination.

This Plywood can be distinguished by the alternating color layers within the two surfaces. Poplar is lightweight, so the Plywood bends and warps easily. The overall density of the Plywood is relatively low. Durability may be compromised in Indian conditions, but the bright side is that both Eucalyptus and Poplar are borer resistant. Hence, if you do not expect to put lots of weight and pressure on the woodwork, then this is a good option for you, even in terms of budget.

Figure 18: **Alternate Plywood is easily identifiable, with each alternating layer having alternating color - Reddish and Whitish.**

My take: Good for commercial spaces like offices. Cheaper compared to other Plywood. Suitable for constructions where lots of weight on the woodwork is not expected.

Poplar Plywood

Poplar is a low-density timber. This variety of Plywood is 100% poplar. It is low-density and lightweight. It is not very durable, and it has low screw holding and shear strength.

Due to its weaker disposition, Poplar Plywood is one of the cheapest Plywood options available in India. Since it may be pretty cheap, it is tempting to buy it for your interior construction works, but unless for very small jobs, it is highly recommended to avoid it.

My Take: Avoid as long-term durability is very low.

Birch Plywood

This is a very premium high-quality Plywood, and there has been an increased demand for Birch-based Plywood in India of late. Since it is found in Russia and Finland, it is not ideal for Indian climatic conditions, but the woodwork looks quite classy in temperature-controlled environments. It is completely imported right now and sold in India through various traders.

My take: As mentioned above, not entirely suitable for Indian conditions. Use it for indoor woodwork if you want a rustic look with minimum polishing. It is a preferred option for high-end OEM furniture manufacturers for very specific applications.

Beech Plywood

This innovative variety of Plywood has been developed in India. The inner layer of the Plywood is made of Eucalyptus hardwood, and the top layers comprise of the European beech veneer. This gives you durable Plywood with immense aesthetic appeal. The most significant advantage with this Plywood is that you do not need to use a laminate but straight away polish or stain it into any color you want. We have personally delivered some fantastic results with this grade of Plywood, especially for customers who wished to have a Veneered look and feel but with a much lower budget.

Figure 19: Furniture made from Beech Plywood that was polished and no laminate was used.

My take: This is good, Plywood. You need not use laminates; and instead, this Plywood can be straightaway polished and provide a fat better value for money than purchasing plywood and laminate separately.

Rubberwood Plywood

This is cheap-grade Plywood. It is made in the factories in Kerala, which has emerged as a large manufacturing hub for cheap grade Plywood. This Plywood is made of plantation timber available in large quantities. Nonetheless, it has a very low resistance to insect infestation, especially Borer.

My take: I specifically do not recommend this variety of Plywood.

Summary Chart

	Gurjan	Hard wood	Mixed H/W	Alternate	Poplar	Rubber wood	Birch	Beech
Strength	Very High	High	Medium	Low	Very Low	Very Low	Very High	High
Price	₹₹₹₹₹₹	₹₹₹₹	₹₹₹	₹₹	₹	₹	₹₹₹₹₹	₹₹₹₹
Density (kg/m3)	710	650	550	450	350	350	680	650
Made in India	Yes	Yes	Yes	Yes	Yes	Yes	No	Yes
Can be polished for aesthetic appeal	No	No	No	No	No	No	Yes	Yes
Value for Money	No	Yes	No	No	No	No	Yes	Yes
Termite Resistance	High	High	Medium	Low	Low	Very Low	Medium	Medium
Screw Holding Strength	Very High	High	Medium	Medium	Low	Very Low	Very High	High
Availability	Low	High	High	Very High	High	High	Low	Low
Propensity to Warp/ Bend	Very low	Very Low	Medium	Medium	High	High	Very Low	Low

Chapter 9

VARIOUS GRADES OF PLYWOOD

You select the grade of the Plywood according to your construction needs or whether you need Plywood for exterior or interior needs. The possibility of the woodwork getting exposed to water and for how long also impacts the grade of the Plywood.

The different layers of Plywood are bonded using glue or resin. Along with the type of wood species used for manufacturing the Plywood, the type of glue used also determines its strength and durability. The glue also has a direct impact on what climate your woodwork can withstand, how resistant it is to a termite infestation, and how strongly it holds the screws. The Plywood manufactured using the phenol formaldehyde resin can withstand being immersed in boiling water for up to 72 hours without getting damaged. It also has higher screw holding and nail shear strength.

The Plywood of this grade is dipped in a greenish/ brownish solution to make it look different from the regular Plywood. Having said that, just because a Plywood has been dipped in such a solution does not necessarily make it Marine Grade. I will explain below why.

The most common terms used for the Plywood grades are Boiling Waterproof (also known as BWP, IS 710, PF, and Marine Grade), Commercial grade Plywood (also known as CWR, Moisture Resistant, IS 303), and Fire-Retardant Plywood.

Let's know their differences.

Boiling Waterproof/Marine-grade Plywood

This grade of Plywood is also known by many other names such as IS 710, BWP Plywood, just Marine, and PF grade Plywood. As mentioned above, PF stands for phenol formaldehyde, and you can dip it in boiling water for 72 hours without it going bad. This makes it ideal for long-lasting woodwork.

The 72 hours boiling waterproof test means that the long-term durability is very high, and so is the screw holding strength.

My take: This is the preferred option for any form of long-lasting woodwork solution, especially in our country, where high humidity and seasonal changes are the norm.

Beware of the marine grade fraud

Since this is top-grade Plywood, many customers want to use it for woodwork, making them vulnerable to falling victim to fraud. Often, low-grade material is fraudulently marketed and sold as marine-grade Plywood. Always ready to walk the extra mile to ensure good quality Plywood for my customers, it often pains me to see people being hoodwinked, and I would like to share an insight that can save you from being defrauded.

I would quickly like to add that you should always deal with a branded company because for a branded company, committing such fraud is not worth it. They have spent years building their brand, and they would not like to tarnish it merely to make a few quick bucks.

With this out of the way, let us find out how to find if the marine grade Plywood that you are about to purchase is genuine or not.

Take a small piece of the Plywood – do not use the trade sample because the trade sample is normally genuine – and keep it immersed in water for 2-3 days. I know this is cumbersome, but believe me, it is worth the effort. After all, if you want to use marine-grade

Figure 20: Commercial Plywood marked as Waterproof Plywood was kept in water for 3 days. At the end, the ply delaminated which would never happen with a genuine waterproof ply

Plywood and paying good money for it, you want to make sure that you are going for the real deal, no?

After three days, if the piece of the Plywood is still intact without any signs of spoiling, bloating, deforming, or discoloring, it is genuine marine-grade Plywood. Otherwise, maybe you need to look somewhere else.

Commercial Plywood/MR Grade

MR means Moisture Resistant. It is manufactured using the urea formaldehyde resin and has a weaker disposition than the BWP grade Plywood. You can keep it immersed in room temperature water for 8 hours without spoiling it.

The overall bonding of this grade of plywood is lower and hence so is the durability. Yes, it is cheaper than the BWP grade Plywood, but you get high-quality Commercial Grade Plywood depending on the raw material used to manufacture.

The lower bonding strength of the resins also means that this grade of material has a lower screw holding strength and is better suited to low moisture, dry climate areas, or commercial spaces.

My take: This grade is typically preferred for large-scale commercial use or purely financial reasons.

Fire Retardant Plywood

This Plywood is known for its fire resistance properties. Unlike other grades of Plywood, Fire Retardant Plywood has a slower burn rate. Treated with various chemicals to achieve this phenomenon, Fire Retardant Plywood will provide you precious minutes to escape a fire before burning down. For example, it takes approximately 30-35 minutes for this Plywood to catch fire and a further

20 minutes to burn. Thus, allowing you crucial time to escape. This is an ideal Plywood option if you are looking for something that does not catch fire easily.

My take: Fire Retardant Plywood also has Boiling Water Proof properties and, coupled with extra protection, is an excellent option to consider for your home or office.

Chapter 10

BLOCKBOARDS: A COMPLEMENTARY OPTION TO PLYWOOD

I find Blockboards quite fascinating, but I consider them as complementary products to Plywood and not a substitute. You can use Blockboards along with Plywood, but Blockboards Plywood cannot completely replace Plywood.

A significant difference between Plywood and Blockboards: Blockboards, as the name suggests, are made of solid blocks of wooden battens sandwiched between thick wood veneer layers. In Plywood, layers or veneers of wood are glued together. Both are combined using high pressure and temperature.

Why do I say that you should use Blockboards as complementary material to Plywood? The wooden battens inside a Blockboard may have gaps between them. Hence, Blockboards are not suitable for horizontal construction works. For example, if you are building a cupboard or a shelf, do not use a Blockboard to make the shelves where you plan to store stuff. The board may break. Since Plywood does not have such gaps, it is stronger than a Blockboard when it comes to bearing weight horizontally.

On the other hand, Blockboards are perfect for vertical construction works. They are suitable for paneling or cupboard shutters. If you are constructing a wooden structure that is 7 feet or higher, it is better to use Blockboard for its greater vertical load-bearing strength.

Are there high-quality Blockboards available?

It depends on what you want to do with them. High-quality Blockboards in India are made from kiln-seasoned pine timber. It means the moisture is drawn out of the wood artificially to make it hard and durable. The absence of moisture also makes it resistant to insect attacks. It also endures climatic changes better.

Most of the good quality pine used for manufacturing Blockboards is imported from New Zealand, Canada, or the USA because this Pine has the least number of dead knots. In India, too good quality pine is available, especially from Meghalaya, but these days, there are some restrictions in the northeast, and hence, the availability is poor.

Figure 21: Best quality of Pine comes from Canada, USA, and New Zealand. India has good quality Pine but only from Meghalaya and is very hard to find now. Himachal Pine is low in quality and used for low grade boards.

Low-quality Blockboards are unseasoned, which means moisture is not drawn from them artificially. These low-quality Blockboards can be made of Pine, mixed hardwood, or Poplar.

These boards deteriorate fast. They are prone to being infested by insects and termites. They also lose shape when the season changes.

Figure 22: Pine has a distinct grain structure that is easily visible. Look out for this type of color and grain when your board is cut to know for sure if it is made with Pine or not.

The table listed below gives you a summary of the comparison between good-quality and poor-quality Blockboards.

Good Quality Blockboards		Poor Quality Blockboards
Seasoning	Kiln Seasoned	Sun-Dried/No Seasoning
Timber	Imported Pine	Mixed Hardwood, Low-Quality Pine, Poplar
Durability	Very High	Low
Warping	Negligible due to proper seasoning	High Chances
Screw holding Strength	High	Medium
Resistance to Termite	High	Very Low

Similar to Plywood, Blockboards come in the same grades – Boiling Water Proof and Moisture Resistant with similar properties and applications.

Chapter 11

CHOOSING BETWEEN PLYWOOD AND BLOCKBOARDS

Surprisingly, there is confusion on this issue not just among the users and laypeople but also among contractors and the design community.

As you have read above, they are of different compositions, and hence, they are different materials. You can use them together, but you cannot replace one with the other.

Blockboards are suitable for vertical constructions because of the higher vertical load-bearing strength. I recommend that you use them for shutters and other vertical applications such as panels, partition walls, and the sidewalls of long cupboards.

Plywood is made with alternating layers of wood veneer, which, although gives it a lot of strength, it creates tension at the corners when applied vertically. Therefore, over time, it can bend/warp in applications higher than 7 feet. And for this reason, most contractors then use aluminum framing to prevent bending and warping– adding further cost to your project.

My take: Whether you want to go with Blockboards, Plywood, or a combination of both depends on your contractor or the availability of good-grade Blockboards. For example, in South and Western India, high-quality Blockboards are not readily available, and most contractors have found a way around this scarcity. Nonetheless, it is a compromise. For ideal construction, both Plywood and Blockboards must be used in conjunction.

Section D

PRECAUTIONS & SUMMARY

Chapter 12

HIDDEN SECRETS OF THE PLYWOOD INDUSTRY

With more than 80% of the Plywood coming from the unorganized sector, it is understandable that identifying counterfeit Plywood and Blockboards can be a daunting task.

Sometimes the customer does not even know that there is a concept of branded and unbranded Plywood. After all, to a layperson, every piece of Plywood seems fine. The ISI mark is there. Some important-looking stamps are there. Company names are printed on the boards. It feels and looks like wood. What could possibly be wrong?

Here is what they do to deceive you (knowingly or unknowingly):

- The product is made to look like a known brand.
- The product is sold under IS 710, whereas it is an MR grade Plywood.

- The product is painted and visually made to look like hardwood but is Poplar or alternative wood.
- Warranty and guarantee are offered with no teeth and no intention to follow through.

Fine, you say. The market is flooded with counterfeit or low-quality Plywood,and for a layperson, it might be challenging to differentiate. How can then one recognize genuine Plywood?

Listed below are a few things you can do.

Products are marked to sound and look like renowned brands

As mentioned above, every company has its unique process of identifying genuine Plywood. If you are dealing with a branded company; they have an extensive sales team. Interact with one of the salespersons and ask about the process of checking genuine Plywood. At our company, we use a QR code and a scratch code on all our products. Using your smartphone, you can find out whether the Plywood that you are purchasing from us is genuine or not.

Products are marked to appear to be a genuine brand

These days, every renowned brand has a significant presence on the Internet. Check out their website, their social media presence, and customer testimonials. Being a renowned brand, they must have supplied Plywood to a large customer base. Again, as already mentioned, every recognized company has an extensive sales network.

Contact one of the salespersons to seek as much information as you want.

Figure 23: Unbranded Plywood is marketed in India to sound like a brand but in reality, is not. In addition, they accompany tall warranty claims, but ask for the full terms and conditions to really know if the warranty claim is hollow or genuine.

Warranty and guarantee a promised but with no substance

Ask for their full terms and conditions. Usually, warranties are mentioned for 21 years or even 50 years, but these are for manufacturing defects. What's the catch?

Manufacturing defects are detected and recognized when your furniture is being made or when your woodwork is being fixed. Defects that can render your woodwork useless do not show at that time. Most of the problems, such as Plywood swelling or getting infested by termites, happen after about a year. By that time, the terms and conditions mentioned in the warranty document no longer apply. Make sure that the warranty covers termite infestation.

In many instances, they mention that warranty does not cover termite infestation but rather covers manufacturing defects. Well, manufacturing defects, if any, are almost always found out at the time of making the furniture and do not have a long-term implication.

Products are sold under IS 710 but are actually of MR grade

As mentioned earlier, get a sample piece of the Plywood you are about to purchase and keep it immersed in water for a couple of days. Every renowned brand makes such ample available for this purpose. If they are reluctant or dillydally, or if they do not give you the Plywood from which you obtained the sample, you know that something is fishy.

After being immersed in water for two days, if the Plywood does not swell or become deformed, it is a genuine product.

Products are painted on the side to make them look as if they are hardwood, whereas they may be Poplar or Alternate wood

Many local Plywood manufacturers varnish their Plywood on the side with red color to make it look like hardwood.

How do you know it is genuine or not?

Here is a simple way to check. Take a piece of the Plywood and look inside. If every layer is white or if alternate layers are red and white, then there is a 90% chance that it is not a genuine product.

Chapter 13

IN A NUTSHELL

To give you as much information as possible, I have covered important points in different sections of the book. Here I will compile all the important points to keep in mind when choosing the ideal Plywood and Blockboard.

- Go for hardwood Plywood that is boiling waterproof.

- For cupboard shutters and vertically elongated applications, choose waterproof, pine-based Blockboards that are treated for sturdiness and termite resistance.

- Clearly go through the terms and conditions. Make sure that you get a guarantee or warranty against the wood spoiling or getting infested by termites.

- Opting for Gurjan wood? Get it tested to make sure that it is genuine Gurjan.

- Want to know if your Plywood is genuinely waterproof? Get a small sample and keep it immersed in water for two days. It should remain intact. Then make sure that you buy the SAME Plywood from where you got the sample.

- Every company that sells branded Plywood has its own genuineness checking process. Please talk with a representative to know what their process is.

I sincerely hope that after reading this book, you are better informed and empowered, and when you purchase your Plywood, you will be able to make the right decisions for your home.

Looking for more information or just want to check out our product range?

Please visit my websites www.plywoodguide.com. Please feel welcome to get in touch. I love to hear from people who are passionate about genuine Plywood.

I like to keep an interactive digital presence. Everyday my team and I answer all queries received from the website to ensure that the consumers get all the information they need.

Love books? Here is good news for you. I am writing another book on finishing material to be used, especially for Decorative Veneers. I am sure you will find that book equally helpful.

All the best for your upcoming woodwork. And do keep in touch.